Away With Words

Alison Turner

BookLeaf
Publishing

Presentation by *BookLeaf Publishing*

Web: www.bookleafpub.com

E-mail: info@bookleafpub.com

ISBN: 9789357211536

First edition 2023

DEDICATION

For Pat,

You said you would like to read some of my poems one day :) .

PREFACE

If I could only have one thing for the rest of my life, it would be my words.

One Year Down

My body craves poison
Click. Twist. Pop

Every sunny day
Click. Twist. Pop

My mouth yearns the taste
Click. Twist. Pop

Of the substance that I hate
Click. Twist. Pop

Dumb Love

I cared for you,
With every inch of my body

I loved you twice as much

I trust in God,
That he has a plan

But that doesn't mean it doesn't suck.

Weight of Life

A young lady
Sat on the sand
Watching the waves crash in sequence

She craves the flow,
The system of life,
Which she finds that only the beach gives

Her heart yearns for adventure
New shoulders, less pressure
And a hand to guide her through it

But this lady on the sand
With her life on demand
Has a role that she must commit

Her sister needs her there,
the road to repair
And for that, the pressure is worth it

Cloud Nine

Dating you was like floating on a cloud;
Weightless,
heightened,
euphoric

Until a foot slipped, and I fell in the cloud;
Dense,
foggy,
grey

With no support below me.

History

Those brown eyes I loved
Are now ones I don't know

And my mind is filled with facts
About the boy I should let go

A Recipe for a Well Lived Life;

- someone who looks at you like you're the whole world

- someone to look at like they're the whole world

One Last Time

I think I'll always be crossing my fingers, hoping
that you hold me
One last time

And then,
When you let go
I'll be hoping that there's another
'One last time'

City Life

Like a deck of cards,
You're shuffled around.

Slip through the cracks,
And never be found.

Squint of Love

Your eyes,
Meeting someone else's
With the same happy
Squint of love

Restoration

Ocean breeze,
With salty scents

Caress my body,
With innocence

Crow-feet wrinkles

I want to be standing on a beach,
With a baby on my hip,
And crow-feet wrinkles by my eyes

Smile

I want to be
Valued for my words
And loved by my smile

Loved to be loved

Elke looked at Tom unlike anyone had ever
looked at someone before.

She looked at him with wonder;
Wonder of what each word really meant.

She looked at him with complexity;
Like she could spend an entire lifetime trying to
understand this boy and not once get bored.

She looked at him with adoration;
Staring into his eyes that stay forever engrained
in her heart.

Tom looked at Elke with boyish wonder.
He looked at her with promise
And warmth.

But I think he was really just looking at his own
reflection in her eyes.

Elke loved to love.
Tom loved to be loved.

Sleep deprived

I try to stop my thoughts
And tell myself it's fine

But I miss your face
And the nights that never died

A letter to my future self

Your heart isn't broken.

It’s not broken after your mum chooses alcohol over you.

It’s not broken after your dad speaks badly to you.

And no matter how badly it hurts, it’s not broken after your first love leaves you.

A broken heart can’t love like yours does.

Loss

Every piece of my body was once warmed by you,
And is now left again cold.

I'm not just mourning the loss of you,
It's the loss of everything I loved whilst loving you.

Growing Up

When I was nine years old,
Growing up meant 'high pony's' that swung
side-to-side when I walked

At ten years old,
It was slotting 'like' in
Whenever I talked

Age eleven was boy bands

And twelve,
Holding hands

Thirteen was first kisses,
All planned

When I was fourteen
I craved routine
To keep my life in order

At fifteen growing up
Was growing less
Smaller...
Smaller...
Smaller...

Age sixteen,
I fell in love
And that meant I was wiser

But seventeen
I fell apart
Because older isn't brighter

Growing up,
I've come to realise
Doesn't follow a timeline set

It's taking life as it is,
Both the love and regret

It's learning without speaking
And speaking without lie

Growing up is ever changing,
And the years will fly on by

Closure

You saw that you had taken everything from me

But you still wanted more.

www.ingramcontent.com/pod-product-compliance
Lightning Source LLC
Chambersburg PA
CBHW051721130826
49812CB00034B/1283
9789357211536